MONSTER POETRY

RHYMES FROM SCOTLAND

Edited By Donna Samworth

First published in Great Britain in 2018 by:

YoungWriters

Young Writers
Remus House
Coltsfoot Drive
Peterborough
PE2 9BF
Telephone: 01733 890066
Website: www.youngwriters.co.uk

Book Design by Ashley Janson

SB ISBN 978-1-78896-724-2
Printed and bound in the UK by BookPrintingUK
Website: www.bookprintinguk.com
YB0371H

FOREWORD

Young Writers was created in 1991 with the express purpose of promoting and encouraging creative writing. Each competition we create is tailored to the relevant age group, hopefully giving each child the inspiration and incentive to create their own piece of writing, whether it's a poem or a short story. We truly believe that seeing it in print gives pupils a sense of achievement and pride in their work and themselves.

Our latest competition, Monster Poetry, focuses on uncovering the different techniques used in poetry and encouraging pupils to explore new ways to write a poem. Using a mix of imagination, expression and poetic styles, this anthology is an impressive snapshot of the inventive, original and skilful writing of young people today. These poems showcase the creativity and talent of these budding new writers as they learn the skills of writing, and we hope you are as entertained by them as we are.

CONTENTS

THE POEMS

Grizalinaa And Her Boring Homework

I woke up one morning
And was told a serious warning,
That, if I don't get up,
I will not get a cute pup!

So I jumped out of bed and greeted,
But I did not get treated,
So I went downstairs and had my breakfast
And I remained steadfast.

So when I had finished,
I had loads of stuff unfinished,
Like homework and all that stupid stuff,
But my mother just replied, "Tough!"

So I had to go and get my homework,
But instead, I decided to do my artwork,
My father came up to my room and said,
"Your sister is going to be fed!"

I didn't get what he said because,
Wait, I need to pause...
He said that to me but I don't get it,
But I can't admit.

I did my maths first,
Though I just failed so I burst,
Could life get any worse?
Everything in this verse
Is just like a story!

When it was time for popcorn,
It was as if I weren't born,
I shouted and shouted
And I found out that they had voted!

I jumped back upstairs growling and growling
And then I remembered I had to go bowling,
But I thought they were wrong in the head,
When I looked close in the mirror, I was red.

I tried the methods my sweet teacher taught me,
That if you hover like a bumblebee,

You will then see what we all see,
Then probably you would go to sea!

The rhyme didn't help me at all,
I then decided to go and get a ball,
My father and mother came to my room
And then I thought I was in such a doom!
I bent my head down and pretended to calculate
And I ended up to meditate.

Stephanie Chiezita Nwaopara (9)

Lollipops The Cyclops

I'm Lollipops,
The evil cyclops,
I'm a bad little beast,
Looking for a feast,

If you say I'm cute,
You'll change your mind when I kick you with my foot!
Children Pie's my favourite meal,
I love the taste and even the squishy feel.
So, if you're a child out there,
Watch your step and beware!

From my horns to my eye,
You know I'm going to make you cry,
I am very, very hairy,
And I hope you think I'm scary.

From my claws to my feet,
When you see me your heart will quickly beat,
My teeth aren't very attractive,
When you run away, you'll be active.

I'm Lollipops,
The evil cyclops.
I'm a bad little beast,
Looking for a feast,
So, if you're a child sat there,
Watch out and... *beware!*

Luke Kelly (10)
All Saints' Primary School, Airdrie

Fluffy My Monster

I am cute and fluffy,
I am very cuddly too,
My hair is very puffy,
And I am very new.
I like to give cuddles,
I am very friendly too,
I like to jump in puddles,
And I only have one shoe.
I've got one eye in the centre of my face,
I brush my teeth with my three arms,
So they're never a disgrace.
When I walk, I always leave a trace,
My home planet is a pink and purple place.
I like to play, cuddle and dance,
I love to sleep, especially all day.
But when I dance, I fly to France,
So please do ask to play.

Leah Thomson (11)
All Saints' Primary School, Airdrie

Milly The Magical

Hi, my name is Milly,
And I have magical powers.
My fur is as red as a rose,
And I really love to pose.
I love eating worms,
And snakes with mice.
In the water I make flames dance,
I make frogs still and snails prance.
My light turquoise hair,
As soft as soft can be.
I am very nice,
I love a little spice,
I love flying
High in the air.
I can turn invisible,
And I am also invincible.

Jay Sweeney (11)
All Saints' Primary School, Airdrie

Pinkou

(Haiku poetry)

I have a monster,
And she's a magic monster,
Her name is Pinkou.

Pinkou is fluffy,
She is a talking monster,
She can cuddle me.

Pinkou is spotty,
She's also very furry,
And she is so nice.

Sophia Phillips (6)
All Saints' Primary School, Airdrie

Furry

(Haiku poetry)

I have a monster,
She is a magic monster,
Her name is Furry.

Furry is friendly,
She is a talking monster,
She likes to hug me

Furry is purple,
She always has lipstick on,
And has orange spots.

Orlaith Suzanne McMullen (6)
All Saints' Primary School, Airdrie

Fluffy

My monster is green,
My monster is called Fluffy,
She is so friendly.
She is so fluffy,
My monster is so stripy,
Fluffy has one eye.
She has a square tail,
She has really floppy ears,
She is the cutest!

Amelia Bryden (7)
All Saints' Primary School, Airdrie

Chubby

My monster is white.
My monster is called Chubby,
And she is spotty.
Chubby is friendly,
She is very, very cute,
I love her so much.

Lily Hamill (6)
All Saints' Primary School, Airdrie

Fato

(A haiku)

He likes cake to eat,
He eats children from school too,
And dark chocolate!

Rhys Mullen (6)
All Saints' Primary School, Airdrie

Funny

(A haiku)

My monster has spots,
He likes to eat big children,
He loves to eat sweets.

Marc Antony McDermott (6)
All Saints' Primary School, Airdrie

Scwash The Monster

Beware, oh beware, for he may scare,
the monster with a creepy stare,
He will sneak up and give you a fright,
But there's an upside to your fight,
He only comes out in the dead of night.
That eye, that eye, that lonely eye
With that eye, that only eye,
He will spy you in the sky
With those deadly horns,
He will spike you,
Just like deadly thorns,
They will pierce your skin
Lightning thin.
Beware, oh beware,
For Scwash will always be there...

Callum Crocker (10)
Auchtergaven Primary School, Bankfoot

A Monster Called Bot

Have you ever met a monster,
A monster bright and green,
Oh, but he is never seen,
He lives up a tall tree,
Where he's always spying on me.
Have you ever met a monster,
A monster small and round,
He's called Bot,
But he's just a dot,
People say he's cute, but he's really not.
Who will he be watching?
Will it be you?

Ellie Marsh (10)
Auchtergaven Primary School, Bankfoot

Furry The Monster

My monster, Fuzzy, is purple and blue,
And he has come a long way to visit you,
He travelled through space, a great distance,
Tossing and turning, churning and burning, until...
He crash-landed on a farm,
But to you, he means no harm.

Ryan O'Connor (10)
Auchtergaven Primary School, Bankfoot

John The Alien

John the alien was scary,
He was scaring everyone in town.
John the alien was being scary
John the alien was frightening all the people in the street.
John the alien was scared of the people.
John was scared because he lost his family,
They left him behind because they couldn't keep him,
He was crazy and was driving everyone mad!

Joseph Hutchison Marshall (8)
Banchory Primary School, Tullibody

Staying In A Sunny Paradise!

Princess Angel is kind,
She likes to find stuff,
She smells like the ocean,
And doesn't like devotion.
She tries her best,
To keep everyone calm and kind.
She loves being everyone's friend,
She is very good,
And not very rude.
She flies all day,
Without delay,
She lives in a paradise.

Sophie Stevenson (8)
Banchory Primary School, Tullibody

Spider Cat Jello

Spider Cat Jello,
SCJ for short,
From Uranus,
Short, yummy, fun,
He saves children from a fall,
"Hip hip hooray for Spider Cat Jello!"

Aeren Abbott (9)
Banchory Primary School, Tullibody

Fluffy Fuzz The Friendly Monster

Fluffy Fuzz was born in space on Mars,
Fluffy Fuzz is as yellow as the sun,
He is short,
he has fluffy fur,
He has big black eyes,
His tail is long,
His voice is cute,
His mouth is tiny.
Fluffy Fuzz liked hanging out by himself,
So he had no friends,
But he landed on Earth with all the humans.
Then, all of a sudden,
A human brought him to his house,
He wouldn't let him go,
Until he had answered all his questions.
The window was open,
And he flew out the window,
He was free, then he said, "Woo hoo! I am free!"
Everyone came around him because he was singing,

No one knew that he was secretly a singer,
Then he was a billionaire and a real singer.

Chloe Coyle (8)
Bonhill Primary School, Bonhill

The Rainbow

Cotton was born in a rainbow,
She had pink, fluffy skin,
And black, liquorice eyes,
And white, cotton wings,
Like fluffy snow.
Cotton had lots of friends,
Her best friend is Bubblegum the marshmallow.
One day, Cotton and Bubblegum went on an adventure,
Up to the sky,
They made a friend called Coco,
Coco was secretly evil.
She had red, fluffy skin and blue eyes,
And she likes to drink blood,
But she only does it secretly,
And has black wings,
That are as dark as coal.
But Cotton didn't know Coco was evil,
But just then, Bubblegum told Cotton,
Cotton and Bubblegum flew away,

And then, Coco came back,
And she was so nice,
They were all friends again...

Kallie Thomson (8)
Bonhill Primary School, Bonhill

Fluffy The Monster

Fluffy came from a rainbow,
She was from the colours purple and blue,
They matched her tail.
Fluffy was a unicorn cat that could fly,
Her beautiful, velvet wings flapped together,
Then apart in the sky,
With rainbow clouds so high.
When she went to fly,
Her best friend came by,
And said, "Hello," very happily,
And then continued on her journey.
Fluffy wondered where she was going.
There was her enemy, Addison,
She was a bully,
She always had that cheeky smile,
She gave Fluffy a dirty look,
As cheeky as a chimp.
Her fur looked soaking wet,
But it was rough,
And every time others passed,
They screamed as loudly as an elephant.

Ellie Andrew (7)
Bonhill Primary School, Bonhill

The Fallout!

Once there was a monster called Mrs Cuddly,
And she came from outer space.
She had friends called Kayla, Evie, and Sky,
They were very funny and goofy and very kind.
They always had her back, but then, they fell out,
They didn't talk to each other.
Also, they didn't even look at each other,
They were always trying to make the others jealous.
But they went up to space,
they didn't know that they were going to meet,
They went up to Saturn then...
They saw each other and ran over,
and had a group hug.
"I love you guys," said Sky
The next day, Mrs Cuddly went to see her husband,
and kissed him goodbye and went to work.

Carrie Park (9)
Bonhill Primary School, Bonhill

The School Bully

Stinky Fuzz was born in a bin,
He didn't really like it there.
He had big ears,
He had small hands,
his house was a bit smelly,
But he was getting used to it.
Before the first day at school,
His mum packed his lunchbox,
"Have a good day, Sweetie,"
Said Stinky Fuzz's mum.
His mum's voice sounded,
as loudly as a lion roaring,
In fact, it was even louder,
Than a lion roaring.
He didn't like anyone at his school,
And he bullied everyone.
Someone tried to bully Stinky Fuzz,
But he turned into a giant,
And destroyed the school,
But it was just a dream.

Kayleigh Munley (8)
Bonhill Primary School, Bonhill

The Return Of The Zip-Zoop

One day I saw something,
It was big and it had wings,
Five eyes and some hurtful horns,
The Zip-Zoop was his name.
He was born in the Russian mountains,
And he was very dangerous,
Nobody knew what it was,
I went to see it,
And it wasn't very pleasant.
It scratched and ate,
Never showered, ate raw meat,
He lived in a super stinky cave,
He attacked me with his talons,
And *bang!* The cave shook,
I shivered with fear,
And *bang!* The cave began to crumble.
The Zip-Zoop froze,
I saw a figure,
Who could it be?

Jack Biglie (8)
Bonhill Primary School, Bonhill

Lofey's Rainbow Adventure

Once there was a monster called Lofey,
She lived in a rainbow.
When a rainbow came out, she would too.
She didn't like living in a rainbow,
In fact, she hated it,
So she made a plan to disguise herself as a person,
She had a master plan to get evil back on her side.
Lofey is only thirteen,
She is the rainbow, evil queen.
In the rainbow everyone is scared of her,
When she came out of the rainbow,
She was so powerful.
She cast an evil spell,
On everyone in the whole wide world,
They never saw the light of day again.

Eva Murdoch (9)
Bonhill Primary School, Bonhill

Evil Bop

BB Bop was from a disc,
BB Bop was very hairy, fluffy, and very small,
BB Bop had dark blue eyes, and an irresistable face.
He had a friend called CC Swag.
One day, CC Swag was going to perform at a disco,
BB Bop was evil so he locked CC Swag in a cage,
So CC Swag couldn't perform,
And couldn't be more popular or more amazing.
Then BB Bop's dark blue eyes,
Turned into bright red, evil-looking eyes,
"Hee, hee, hee," BB Bop said.

Gracie Wilson (8)
Bonhill Primary School, Bonhill

Pinkie Pie's First Day Of School

It was Pinkie Pie's first day at school.
Pinkie got up for school,
She was so sad because she had no friends,
She didn't know what they would think of her,
But she was pretty, fluffy and clever.
Then it was time for her to go to school.
When she got to school,
All of the girls were being mean to her,
Then she ran off, she was sad as the blue sky,
She hated those girls.
Then a girl came up to her,
She was nice, they became friends.

Kayla McGregor (9)
Bonhill Primary School, Bonhill

The Adventure

Fierce Flyer was born in a basement,
He has smoky white skin, red evil eyes.
He has dark, black wings like coal
Melting in my ears.
He is evil. He likes to drink blood.
He flew out of the basement for an adventure,
He needed to haunt people,
So he could be proud.
He saw people in a house,
He said, "Time to fright,"
They tried to catch him,
But they could not.
He said, "I'll be back,"
And off he flew.

Brooke-Lynn Lynch (8)
Bonhill Primary School, Bonhill

Fluffy Blue

There was a bad, fluffy monster called Fluffy Blue,
And he was so bad.
He had five eyes, black fangs,
And he was naughty,
He had blue fluff and green eyes,
And black ears,
He was so scary, no one liked him,
They didn't talk to him.
One day, Fluffy Blue went to a monster's house,
And broke everything in the house.
Then the monster police came,
Fluffy Blue was in so much trouble.

Rebecca Natasha Maria Murdoch (9)
Bonhill Primary School, Bonhill

Domination Ends The World

Domination was born in an alien egg,
And it crashed on Earth.
He had friends called Bob and Jack,
They were good, but he was bad.
Him and his friends were at the beach,
Swimming in the water.
Domination killed his friend
By dragging him into the water,
He jumped into a human body
With his red eyes.

Warren Lynch (9)
Bonhill Primary School, Bonhill

Lucky Little Monster

Hi, I am Toddles,
I live in a lollipop factory.
I have blue spirals on my body,
I am as slow as a snail,
And I am a tough toddles.
I am purple with blue spirals on my body,
I am a little, crazy creature.
I have an important job in the factory,
As I have to taste test everthing,
So, if you see a little bite mark,
It wasn't me.
I love eating sweets and licking lollies,
I am as cute as a puppy,
And I really want a home,
So I walked to a pet shop,
I hope they accept me in the shop,
So I can get a home.
I am very good,
I will wash the dishes and make dinner.

Finally, I got a great home,
And I love it,
I am the luckiest little monster.

Mia Davidson (10)
Cathkin Primary School, Rutherglen

Bulldo

Bulldo, the terrifying creature
Was born in the depths of Hell.
He was as scary as an evil clown,
But slept like a kitten,
He was hairy and scar-filled,
And as powerful as a bull.
Anyone who decided to fight him,
Was a total fool.
Bulldo was capturing villagers to kill them.
The villagers were prepared and had traps,
They were always prepared every night,
But the beast was too powerful.
He took villagers and ate them every night.
Blood was splashed everywhere,
He was strong, he had a six-pack,
He went up to his car and threw fire sticks,
And he didn't come back.

Riley Holland (10)
Cathkin Primary School, Rutherglen

Untitled

The dragon was born in a volcano
It was a fire dragon
It liked to destroy wagons
It liked to destroy and defeat stuff
And it would not give up
It would keep going
Until it got what it wanted
I guess you could call it the 'big guy'
It hunted down the people
Until it got them to give up their city
Finally he was tired because some people would never give up their city
So the dragon went back to his volcano and gave up.

Paul Paterson (9)
Cathkin Primary School, Rutherglen

The Little Fluffy Monster

Zoe was born in a land of monsters,
She was as cute as a puppy,
And as fluffy as a kitten,
And she was orange as an orange.
She was going to make people smile,
But she met me.
I was on the beach and I was peach,
And I cuddled her,
She said, "Hi, I am Zoe,"
And no everyone loves her,
And she loves going to the pet shop,
To see cute puppies,
Now she lives with me.

Niamh Bell (10)
Cathkin Primary School, Rutherglen

The Legend Of Oggle And Boggle

Born on Good Friday,
Friday the thirteenth,
Oggle and Boggle,
The conjoined monster twins.
Oggle was good as good can be,
Boggle was bad and evil you see.
They lived on a mountain on the highest hill,
With a door to your closet to give you the chills.
When Oggle is asleep, Boggle will creep,
Into the night to give you a fright.
And, while you're dreaming,
You will wake up screaming,
To the sound of scratching and evil laughing.
When the sun comes up, Boggle must run,
That is the end of his nightly fun.
Poor Oggle the Good has no idea,
That Boggle is causing so much fear,
He sleeps through it all without a care,
And wakes to tell Boggle of his nightmare.

Gracie Shorthouse (9)
Craigholme School, Pollockshields

Pongo Puff Was In The Huff

At the stroke of midnight,
I almost had a fright
Over in the corner,
I saw a little mite.
Then I saw him clearly,
He had two pointed ears,
He was about the size of a gnome,
He kind of looked like foam,
With a fluffy tail,
With nails as sharp as knives.
His hair was grey, his eyes were yellow,
And he was trying to play my cello.
As I opened my eyes much wider,
I could see he was a tiny wolf!
Then I asked him, "What's your name?"
He didn't reply, he just poked me in the eye,
Then he shouted in a squeaky voice,
"My name is Pongo Puff,
And I'm no longer in a huff.

All I want to do is play,
All the night and day."
I whispered, "Do not howl
Or my dog will start to growl."
We counted sheep and I fell asleep.
When I awoke, it was no joke,
Pongo Puff was in a huff.

Sophie Cavin (8)
Craigholme School, Pollockshields

The Smelly Mamoo Monster

Smelly Mamoo is smelly, hairy and strong,
He has a huge, hairy nose, smelly toes,
And muscly arms that are very, very long.
He lives on the planet Gymnasium,
Where all the monsters drink milkshakes of plutonium,
This gives him superpowers and a nice, green glow,
But the milkshakes don't taste very nice,
They taste like a sweaty toe.
He loves to play Galactic Football,
With his monster friends,
He thinks he's very good at it,
I nod my head, I pretend.
Smelly Mamoo is funny and naughty,
We have so much fun,
We get up to lots of michief,
And leave lots of mess when we are done.

Smelly Mamoo is the nicest monster you'll ever meet,
Even though he has a loud monster roar,
And very smelly feet. Ew!

Maryam Hussain (9)
Craigholme School, Pollockshields

Slylum

Oh Slylum was a beast! A beast only feared by one.
Who is me, obviously as I'm the one who believes.
It is not visible to the human eye,
But I know in my heart where this beast shall lie.
He lies in a cave near the top of Mount Everest,
No one shall find him, only the cleverest.
Which shall be me, obviously!
I have a secret that's been hidden too long,
And now is the time to confess my wrong.
I know this beast very well, as we are like sisters,
Yes, she's a girl.
So, as my secret shall no longer be a secret,
A bird's wings shall no longer take it,
For I am Slylum!

Lena McBride (9)
Craigholme School, Pollockshields

Chompysaurus

C hompysaurus is my monster,
H e is the best monster ever,
O nly the teachers disagree,
M y monster cuts my homework.
P laytime is his warship,
Y ellow pincers,
S harp as a knife.
A very obedient monster,
U nderstands the hate of homework,
R unning is much more fun,
U nderestimates the use of homework,
S till, he is my friend.

Beth Coles (9)
Craigholme School, Pollockshields

Monster Day

M onsters are scary,
O h no, oh no,
N obody likes them,
S cary monsters,
T ime for bed,
E r, is that a monster under my bed?
R oar! Roar!

ad! Dad! There's a monster under my bed!"

"**A** monster? Are you sure?"
"**Y** es, I am sure because it's right over there!"

Hibah Haq (10)
Craigholme School, Pollockshields

Blubby

The beastly thing lives in a castle,
She is, most likely, a little rascal.
Her job is to be a lovely queen,
But she is certainly not a magical bean,
She has three yellow eyes that glow,
Her wings can fly over a volcano.
A fluffly and sparkly beast she is,
She loves her beautiful mommy's kiss.
2000 fun friends she has,
Their bellies are full of gas!

Haya Choudhry (9)
Craigholme School, Pollockshields

The Funny Monster

I'm a funny monster, I'm never on time,
My jokes are funny but they never rhyme.
My favourite food is spaghetti slime,
I like to jog, but I never have time.
I get so annoyed because I don't know how to rhyme,
I'm never on time because I can't tell the time,
Can you help me tell the time?

Rumaisa Rashid (8)
Craigholme School, Pollockshields

Lyba The Monster

Lyba the monster is pink and blue,
She would love to play with me and you,
In any type of weather,
She can fly like a floating feather.
She is kind and funny,
And likes to eat honey,
She is pretty and lives in a monster city,
But, best of all,
Lyba has the power to shape-shift every hour.

Aairah-Fatima Ali (9)
Craigholme School, Pollockshields

Smiley!

S miley creates fun wherever he goes,
M iserable people get rid of their woes,
I honestly think a smile makes things better,
L ike when you get a good report letter,
E ven though you feel a bit down,
Y ou just turn your frown upside down.

Olivia Dickson (9)
Craigholme School, Pollockshields

Robot Monster

R obot Monster went on riding
O n his bike. "It's time to go to
B ed," said Mum Robot, so Robot Monster
O pened the door to home and
T wenty-two of his friends were there.

M um brought in the cake and he blew
O ut the candles
N ext, Dad opened the door,
"**S** urprise!" said Dad
T here were more presents waiting at the door.
"**E** rrr," said Robot Monster
"**R** obot Monster?" said Robot Mum...

Ernest Pazdan (8)
Dyce School, Dyce

Scary Selbie

S cary Selbie is as scary as
C an be. His favourite food is
A pples that are green.
R yan is Scary Selbie's best friend.
Y ou'd better get out of the volcano.

S cary Selbie loves the
E arth because it's so bright and shiny.
L illy, his dog, is as fluffy as a ball of fluff.
B alloons make Scary jump so high in the sky
I n Candy World. "What on Earth are you doing on an
E lephant?" said his mum.

Lexie Selbie (8)
Dyce School, Dyce

Monsters

C andy Cuddles is a very
A mazing monster, she is
N ever mean to her
D og. Her dog's name is
Y oyo, and she is very cuddly and she is very sweet.

C andy's dog cuddles dog toys all day, she
U ses her toys to sleep.
D ogs are cute and very small,
D ogs are very tiny, they're very
L ittle. Candy Cuddles loves dogs.
E llie, Candy Cuddles' friend, has a
S uper dog too.

Lexi Murray (8)
Dyce School, Dyce

Flame And The Cat

M y monster likes cats so he got
O ne and the cat was very
N aughty so he put the cat to
S leep and he watched TV for
T he rest of the day. The next day,
E agles were screaming so he called the cat
R ose and they lived happily ever after.

Hernandez Bruzco (7)
Dyce School, Dyce

The Monster Ashley

A shley is as colourful as can be,
S he is beautiful and nice and
H as a fluffy coat. She
L ikes lollipops, she's cute, and her
E yes are like a tropical sunset.
Y esterday I went up to Monster Land to see her.

Emily Kirsten Henderson (7)
Dyce School, Dyce

Stripey

S tripey, isn't that
T rendy but he likes the colours
R ed, orange, and blue like his eyes.
I love the special
P ancakes that Stripey makes
E very day.
Y oung people like Stripey, especially Billy.

Milly Fawns
Dyce School, Dyce

The Great Adventurer

B en Baker is as
E asy to see as Flash, Ben is never
N asty

B en is really
A mazing
K aty is a new friend
E mily is another new friend
R icky too.

Eilidh McDonald (7)
Dyce School, Dyce

Dangel

E nourmous flames coming from a pot.
I nterestingly, the Devil was eight and the
G ate to Heaven was open,
H e had two horns but
T oday, he has one.

Archie Skinner (8)
Dyce School, Dyce

Spaghetti Confetti

Her fur looks like spagetti with little bits of confetti,
She is very small, but her family is tall,
She always eats cake, but never touches steak.
Confetti loves to race, but rarely gets a place,
She loves to eat jelly, while watching the telly,
She has a pig, she also loves to dig.
Confetti loves to run, and to also have fun,
She has three eyes, but that's no surprise,
She loves to go to bed with her pet pig, Ted.

Jasmin Todd (11)
High Mill Primary School, Carluke

Monster Friend

I see a dark figure in the shadows,
I smell rotting fish with eggs and cake,
I hear leaves crunching at every step the creature makes.
I can taste the rotten fish bodies from a distance.
I feel goosebumps going up my arms,
I can feel eyes on me in a creepy way,
I see a beast coming out of the shadows,
His name is Shadow.
He looks lonely, sad, but he is happy to see me,
For some weird reason.

Leahmarie Martin (11)
High Mill Primary School, Carluke

A Monster In My Garden

In my garden, I met a monster,
So cute and fun, he likes to run.
I felt his fur, so soft and smooth,
He likes to show me his groovy moves.
He dances around and has some fun,
Fuzzy is my number one.
He is fluffy and stuffy, he looks like a teddy,
But I like him just the way he is,
For he is just my Fuzzy.
He is short and clever, never on the run,
Fuzzy helps everyone.

Becky Williamson (10)
High Mill Primary School, Carluke

Friendly Freddy

Once there was a monster named Friendly Freddy,
He was five and had lots of friends already.
Freddy was tall and had lots of fur,
Plenty of friends, all of them looked up
Lost for words, they all called out,
"Freddy look up!" Without a doubt,
It was a meteor.
They ran for miles.
Inside the little, candy cottage.
They heard a bang!
Was it safe?

Aiden Isik (12)
High Mill Primary School, Carluke

Giff's Day Out

This poem follows
A griffin called Griff,
Prancing in the valleys,
Singing a riff.
He came across two buildings,
He went into one of them,
That's where his quest began.
Griff heard his parents,
Or maybe just one,
He definitely isn't having fun.

Oliver Isik (10)
High Mill Primary School, Carluke

Mr Twitch

Just pour the potion, flip the switch,
And out pops Mr Twitch.
Mr Twitch is from Finland,
He grew up in a village called Binland.
Mr Twitch is fluffy, fluffy as can be,
And since he has four eyes, he can definitely see.
Mr Twitch is funny, he has the greatest jokes,
But when you get the chocolate,
He is a different bloke.
Mr Twitch's brow is as big as can be,
But when it falls off, he canny even see.
Mr Twitch is popular, he has many friends,
But when it comes to writing,
He will not share his pens.
Now it is time for me to go,
Say goodbye and hug him slow,
Because, with Mr Twitch, you'll never know...

Cara Farrell (11)
Holy Name RC Primary School, Oakley

Friends

Hi, I'm a bluebird and my name is Titan,
I'm a happy bird, I'm going to make your day brighter
Let's be friends, besties,
And go to a land away from all the nasties.
Let's go! Sit on my back, let's go there,
Peaceful, wonderful, look, a horse,
A leopard, a bear!
We're over the seas, I'm sweating
I'm hairy and really weary,
But we're best friends and that's what friends do
We're finally there, look, cats miaow,
Dogs woof and cows moo,
We're there! There's so much to do!

Matthew Kasinski (11)
Holy Name RC Primary School, Oakley

Puffy Poppy's Crazy Moment

Puffy Poppy is crazy,
And even a bit lazy,
And different phases,
And also lots of faces.
She likes red, yellow and blue,
And sometimes dark colours too,
She likes sparkly things,
And even sings.
She comes from Fluffy Puffy Sparkle Land,
She wishes she was in a band,
She is a bit crazy,
She smells like a daisy.
Puffy Poppy can be really silly,
She likes to get dizzy,
She spilled something fizzy,
All over a boy called Billy.

Amy Mcmanus (10)
Holy Name RC Primary School, Oakley

Durpy The Wild Monster

There is a monster and he was in a shop.
This little girl came and, *pop*,
She fell in love with him.
She bought him and walked out,
She was so happy and he was too,
The monster's name was Durpy,
She'd named him.
They went home,
She took him into bed.
By the morning, the monster moved,
from her arms to her head,
She went for breakfast.
When she came back, he was gone,
She looked under the bed,
And he was there!

Maia Wilson (11)
Holy Name RC Primary School, Oakley

The Tree Wagon Dragon

Harrington the dragon lives in a wagon,
Peacefully alone in a park.
This little dragon that lives in a wagon,
Likes doing yoga in a tree in the dark.
The four eyes on his head,
Hang on by a thread,
But they often fall out,
When he's asleep in bed.
The fire he breathes is fierce and bold,
Although he doesn't look it, he's dreadfully old.
Harrington loves his vegetarian feast
Of corn and berries, fresh from the east.

Scarlett Louise Murray (11)
Holy Name RC Primary School, Oakley

The Hot Dog Monster!

"Under my bed!"
Said the little sausage head,
He came out from under my bed,
And jumped on my head,
And I flicked him off and said,
"Get to your bed!"
And the little sausage head,
Went back to his bed.
Then I said,
"Don't come back again!"
Then the little sausage head
Went straight to my bed,
Then he broke a leg.
Then the little sausage head,
Never came back again!

Amy Renton (11)
Holy Name RC Primary School, Oakley

Monster School Save

Monster School is being attacked!
But who's there to save it?
It's Glitch! But how will he do it?
Simple! He'll just use his laser eyes to destroy it
He thought, but that wouldn't work!
"Ha, ha, ha," he said, flying into the darkness
"I can't see!"
"You're not going anywhere!"
"I have blasters!"
"Oh no!"
And Monster School was saved.

Michael Aiden Hickson (10)
Holy Name RC Primary School, Oakley

The Very Sweet Monster

I came into my bedroom and guess what I did see?
A big, tall monster that semmed kind of sweet,
With his big, brown eyes and long, sharp teeth,
His multicoloured body that looked kind of sweet,
His short, black hair and bright red horns,
And his long, fluffy tail, that didn't make me wail.
This monster made me happy, not scared at all,
And little did I know, he would be my best friend,
For the rest of time.

Iona Lee (10)
Holy Name RC Primary School, Oakley

Itching For A Fight

Margo stands right up at night,
As we say, "Don't let him bite!"
Under the bed,
He's been itching for a fight,
With his little legs, he zooms into the night,
He stays in this dark,
Don't make a move,
He flies in the sky.
One, two, three,
He eats up meat,
You hide in your bed, hiding from him,
His friends stay in the dark,
Don't mess with him.

Niamh Foy (8)
Holy Name RC Primary School, Oakley

Spot

Spot is cute, cuddly and nice,
And has no price,
Laughs and giggles wherever she goes,
Never a dull moment with Spot.
Spot loves to travel the world,
And go to Aussie and Japan,
To meet new boys and girls,
New friends wherever she goes.
Spot's favourite place to be,
Is up a tree,
Sleeping.

Chloe Crielly (10)
Holy Name RC Primary School, Oakley

The One I Love

The one I love is daring
He is always loving and caring
His skin is puffy
And his nose is stuffy
His eyes look like a puppy
His legs are rough but his heart is lovely
His friends are huffy
But I love them,
Especially when we boogie.

Brooke Renton (11)
Holy Name RC Primary School, Oakley

Coco And Her Wild Adventure

C ute and soft, cuddly and friendly, tiny and smooth,
O n silly string running, she is so wild and brave,
C ontently running across,
O n a silly string tightrope.

Kali Keren Beveridge (8)
Holy Name RC Primary School, Oakley

The Dangerous Bear

Vicious and deadly,
Lives in the volcano,
Kills other monsters,
It is very deadly,
Whomever will kill this terrible beast?
He murders innocent monsters!

Aaron Edward Hickson (8)
Holy Name RC Primary School, Oakley

The Loner

Once upon a time, in a village down below,
There is a mountain with a cave that glows.
Children can't go up there,
It's not a wise thing to do.
The Loner is there, and he might eat you.
One night, he took a girl from her bed,
And took her to the cave,
And she asked, "Why are you called The Loner?"
"Because I'm lonely, and that's the reason why
I won't eat you, because I'm a vegetarian,
I'm not a barbarian."
"I can be your friend," she said.
Her mum and dad came to the cave,
And The Loner explained why he took their
daughter,
And they all became friends.

Emma May Drummond (7)
Portmoak Primary School, Kinnesswood

Monster Dream

I had a dream that I've never had before,
It was about a monster.
Although the monster was frightening,
He lived in a beautiful cave,
It had lights, animals, flowers, everything
And he had friends, they lived under the ground.
I pictured the monster;
He has pitch-black pupils in five eyes,
A red face that's so scary it looked fake.
So if there's any kind of dream I had in my head,
It would be a monster dream.

Eilidh McGarva (7)
Portmoak Primary School, Kinnesswood

Solitaire

The other day, I was getting ready,
When my dad handed me a strange-looking teddy,
My dad said I could take it to school,
I didn't want to, but I acted cool.
The teddy creeped me out all day long,
Well, I suppose it did give quite a pong!
A pong of cheese and meat you see,
And I appeared with a mysterious scratch on my knee.
All I saw was a solitare card,
The thing had really scratched me hard!
I decided to give the doll away,
I gave it to the teacher right away,
She sold it at the great school fair.
The doll mucked up Jenny's hair,
It's not my problem, I don't care,
See you at school Jenny,
If you make it there!

Jaidyn Neil
Raploch Primary School, Stirling

Sumy The Monster

Sumy the monster is never sad,
She has eight legs and a unicorn horn,
She has three eyes and wings to fly,
And loves to eat corn.
Sumy is rainbow-coloured,
And helps them when they are sad,
Sometimes she's happy,
And sometimes she's bad.
To make people happy,
She does the chicken dance.
Her wings are magical,
And are orange and pink.
Sometimes people get scared,
But Sumy always comes prepared!

Skye Salcedas-Beaton (10)
Raploch Primary School, Stirling

The Friendly Monster

There is a monster in my closet,
And his name is Mr Three Eyes,
He always wears underpants,
And his favourite food is pies.
He is very friendly,
He loves playing with kids,
He has red and blue eyes,
And he wastes his money on bids.
He has four purple legs,
And two bunny ears,
Drool coming from his mouth,
And twenty-two fears.

Xiao Feng Huang (11)
Raploch Primary School, Stirling

The Nightmare Of Slob

In the back of your wardrobe,
There stands a monster called Slob,
He has green and pink stripes,
And has a very bad job.
He sneaks in at night,
And always carries a knife,
You will be scared,
But won't have a fright.
You look in your wardrobe,
And have a fright,
You run away,
And won't sleep the night.

Cee-Jay Marie Letford McGowan (11)
Raploch Primary School, Stirling

Slime Monster

After a long day at school,
Children go to bed,
They pick their favourite teddy,
And start to rest their head.
But nobody knows,
That there's a monster in the night,
So watch out,
Or you might get a fright.
The monster's slimy,
And colourful too,
He'd got a virus,
So you might get the flu.

Armani Jayde Laing (11)
Raploch Primary School, Stirling

The Small Scary Monster

If you're a kid,
Please watch out,
A monster's lurking,
And creeping about.
He's got a pink face,
And six big eyes,
He gives kids a fright,
And you can hear their cries.
When you go to bed,
Keep the lights on,
Or Blurp will come and get you,
And in the morning, you'll be gone.

Dannilynne Boles (10)
Raploch Primary School, Stirling

Super Fluffy Dog

There once was a monster called Super Fluffy Dog,
She liked to save animals all day long,
When you came home, you would find,
A monster who knew right from wrong.
Super Fluffy Dog had the power to fly,
Saving animals while floating in the sky.
This monster is the best,
Better than all the rest.

Danielle McCourt (10)
Raploch Primary School, Stirling

Baby Boo Lingers

My monster has lots of powers
And has forks as fingers
His name is Baby Boo,
And, in the dark, he lingers.
He hides under your bed,
Until you look dead,
And then he comes and tricks you,
And you'll see his eyes glow red.

Tamsin Johnston (11)
Raploch Primary School, Stirling

I'm On The Lucozade

There was a monster,
Who was drunk,
That had one eye,
And looked like a punk.
He loved Lucozade,
His best friend was Floyd,
He ate pies,
And his name was Monster-Boyd.

Oliver Rigg
Raploch Primary School, Stirling

Monster Under My Bed

There's a monster called Gremlin,
That lives under my bed,
What type of monster is she?
I am not quite sure,
But she just arrived there,
I'd have noticed her before.
My mother says there's nothing,
And my father shakes his head.
I guess they don't believe,
In the Gremlin under my bed,
I am sure she is still waiting,
Until I turn out the last light,
And settle on my pillows,
For a very long, dark night.
And when I'm softly, fast asleep,
Out comes Gremlin,
From underneath my bed.
That is when she will creep,
In the morning, my parents will be sorry,
When they find my bed empty,
They'll know they should have listened.

I was speaking truthfully,
And they'll forever mourn the day,
That they simply didn't care,
And will always look under their bed,
Because a monster might be there.

Rejoice Edomwonyi (9)
St Clare's Primary School, Drumchapel

Danger Adventures

Danger and his dragon live in space,
They fly like magic brooms.
Danger doesn't have friends,
But he has Dragon to be with him.
Dragon is giant and fluffy,
Dragon flies like a bee,
Dragon has two heads.
Danger and Dragon flew to Saturn,
Danger was mean to the other monsters.
When Danger and Dragon got to Saturn,
Danger made a fireman,
It was like a snowman,
But it was made out of fireballs.

Julia Tomé Menossi Ramos (9)
St Clare's Primary School, Drumchapel

About Tige

Tige is not bad, he's good,
He really likes his food,
He hangs out with his mates,
He likes bugs, but not snakes.
Sometimes at night,
He and his brothers fight,
When he has his friends round,
His mum shouts, "Keep down the sound!"
At Christmas,
He visits Texas,
Tige is my friend,
We are going to be friends till the end.

Jay Lavelle (9)
St Clare's Primary School, Drumchapel

The Happy Riddle Monster

The little riddle was born in a cave,
Not far from a giant, baby volcano,
All he did was make riddles,
His name was Riddle Diddle Who Likes Piddle.
His friends call him Ridd,
But you can call him Piddle,
His mum embarrassed him,
By calling him Hiddle,
That's why he's so little.
Then he went to lie down,
And take his last piddle.

Canzi Sweeney (11)
St Clare's Primary School, Drumchapel

The Cute Blubber Blubber

C uddles and cheers with no fears,
U nder the bed he fled,
T ucked up in his fur, he did not stir,
E ight years of age, but not in a cage.

B alls of fluff like Wigglytuff,
L ooked at me like he wanted tea,
U nbelievable size, like a prize,
B rown in sight,
B rown without a frown,
E yes that are so wise,
R unning away from the wave.

B ig teeth to eat his beef,
L oud and proud,
U nder cover but not a shover,
B lue water makes him look like an otter,
B ig feet but not for ripping sheets,
E ven size to realise,
R ivers make him shiver!

Lucas Dale (8)
St Monica's Primary School, Pollok

Killer At Midnight

K iller Monster is a bad monster,
I t is your worst nightmare,
L oves to eat human beings,
L oves to drink human beings' blood.
E at, eat, eat! That's all he does,
R eally likes to hunt for people.

M oney tastes like hard, chewy sweets to it,
O nly five foot five.
N ick the monster is his best friend,
S illy and slimy, that's what he is,
T all, very tall, taller than a house,
E very day it eats people,
R eally big and fat.

Mikey Dunlop (8)
St Monica's Primary School, Pollok

Scary Monster

S ilent when you are sleeping,
C areful! He bites!
A t night-time, he's under your bed,
R eady, he likes to strike!
Y ou will scream in your dreams!

M adness and scared, all in one go,
O ne, two three, oh, oh, oh!
N o more time, all you can do is run,
S isters won't hear you, it's too late.
T omorrow you'll be gone.
E nd is right now, don't be afraid.
R ight now, people are looking for you.

Ruby Anne Docherty (8)
St Monica's Primary School, Pollok

Choppy The Bang Gone Monster

He is sloppy, his name is Choppy,
He's all gooey and gloopy.
Choppy trails slime like tails,
And takes a lot of bails,
From monster school.
He is bright green, and made of slime,
He also has red on him, and isn't worth a dime,
Choppy was walking through the forest,
He bit a lady's leg and killed her.
A man knew he was a bad monster,
So he tried to shoot him,
But Choppy ran away,
He caught up with him and shot.
Choppy turned to dust and was gone forever.

Erin O'Donnell (8)
St Monica's Primary School, Pollok

Crook The Monster

The monster was called Crook,
He was reading a book,
Then he got up onto his feet,
Trying to eat,
But he also climbed a tree,
With me!
It went on a bike,
But he struggled because of his spike,
When he sat back down,
He was acting like a clown.
Then it quickly ran away,
But I still wanted to play,
When it came back,
It had a big sack.
To go on a trip,
Around the world in a big ship
I am going to miss the monster,
But it was fun playing with it.

Noël Yash Thakur (8)
St Monica's Primary School, Pollok

Oscar In Darkness

Oscar Monster comes out at night
Before you know it, she is rather polite
One day, someone arrived at her house
Oscar opened the door, she screamed, "It's a mouse!"
She screams so loudly, she woke the whole street
She went inside and had a seat
When it was morning, she saw a hole,
So she said, "I'll go down there, oh no!"
And she disappeared.

Chloe Godfrey (8)
St Monica's Primary School, Pollok

Lola And Me

Once, I went out to play,
And I saw something sparkly,
It was a nice, cute ball,
And it was also small.
It did a dance,
Then started to prance,
It was as quiet as a mouse,
So I let it in my house.
It made a giant riot,
Then everything went quiet,
It disappeared.

Natasha Roberts (8)
St Monica's Primary School, Pollok

Maddie The Nice Monster

Very small, all spiky,
Little stomps at my door,
She has a friend, a boy,
Called Mikey.
The big, hairy ears,
And the big, bushy tail,
She started to cry,
With her little tears.
I made a bed,
With colours for her,
She likes to put,
Her head in it.

Orlaith O'Loughlin
St Monica's Primary School, Pollok

Godzilla

It was a spooky night and the thunder was loud,
Godzilla heard footsteps in his cave,
He went flying out of his cave,
There he was,
A guy with an iPhone.
He looked up very slowly,
He peed his pants,
Well, that's one way to drop an iPhone!

Adam Reid (7)
St Monica's Primary School, Pollok

The Baby Monster Was Outside

Outside I saw an egg,
Something popped out, it was a leg.
It was running, it was stunning,
Then I got tools,
And I made rules.
Under the tree,
The monster found a key,
I called him Jumble,
Because his stomach rumbles.

Ethan Smith (9)
St Monica's Primary School, Pollok

Snollappy

In my wardrobe, it always stinks like dog farts,
I shouted for my dad so he came to clean it,
I opened it and I saw a monster eating darts.
My dad jumped out the window into the pool,
Me and the monster thought it looked cool.
The next day, me and the monster had a talk,
While we were on a walk,
He has one massive eye and one small ear.
On the walk, he said he wanted monsters to live here,
I said, "Really? And how are you going to do that?"
He couldn't think, so it looked like he was huffy.
I tried to change the subject, and said he was fluffy,
But he said he didn't want to be good.
Then he threw an amazing party with disgusting food.

Caylin Campbell (9)
Wilton Primary School, Hawick

Jilly The Sea And Correction Monster

Down at the bottom of the sea,
Right next to the sandy beach,
Lives a monster as wild as can be,
That's Jilly, who'll change the way you teach.

Jilly can be good and bad,
Mostly annoying to everything she sees,
But looks very scary and a little bit mad,
And really likes to tease.

If you get pricked by Jilly's horns,
Then your teacher becomes a monster too,
And you won't have fun at school at all,
'Cause you'll get everything wrong,
No matter what you do!

My school were at the beach,
Suddenly Jilly came out,
Looking like a big, fluffy peach,
Pricking everything without a doubt.

The teachers started changing,
The pupils looked weird as well,
This was all exciting,
Almost like a spell.

This Jilly had one friend,
No one knew who it could be,
Nobody could figure it out in the end,
Little did they know it's me!

I'm the one who sends Jilly out,
To scare everyone away,
So that I could be the only person on Earth,
And for me, that's the best way.

Braedyn MacLeod (9)
Wilton Primary School, Hawick

Metal Bender

One stormy night in a metal quarry,
Came a big, bulky, metallic ogre,
Its name was Metal Bender,
It built its whole body out of metal.
When I woke up,
I saw it on my shed,
It picked up pliers,
And put them on his huge arm.
It stomped over to our cat and kicked it.
When I saw it, I didn't know what it was,
Until it shouted, "Metal Bender!"
I sprinted out.
It looked at me, so I came closer,
Then it let out a mighty roar,
It started chasing me.
I ran into the shed and got a hammer,
It ran in front of me and I leaped past,
And closed the door,
But knew it wouldn't hold long,
So I boarded the door, in hope of stopping it,

The shuffling stopped,
It burst through and grabbed me.
I woke up. It was only a dream!

Conall Dalgleish (9)
Wilton Primary School, Hawick

Maylis

Born in a volcano,
She can creep up on you,
Like you don't know.
There's molten red rock on her body,
Colourful, creepy, crooked eyes,
She transports herself everywhere.
But this time, she'd transported to my door.
When I do my homework,
She goes crazy,
She rips up everything,
And chucks it to the floor with her long tongue.
When I tell my teacher why
my homework isn't done,
She doesn't believe me,
But she can't see the little antenna,
Outside the classroom window.
Naughty Maylis!

Amy Rose Richardson (9)
Wilton Primary School, Hawick

Skull Crusher

In a dark, scary, smelly sock drawer,
As old as my granny,
Lived a devil rock monster,
That couldn't stay on the nice level.
He was called Skull Crusher.
He has a curse,
It made Skull steal every purse.
He ran like a flash to the window,
And jumped out.
Surprisingly, he survived.
He saw a pool so he dived in,
He almost drowned, but he didn't,
He was as wet as the swimming pool.
He liked maths and needed a bath,
He looked once more,
He opened the gate,
And found a date.

Lachlan Beukes (10)
Wilton Primary School, Hawick

Rocky

Rocky lives under my bed,
His one eye is green and red,
But it came out to stalk,
At the same time the clock,
Struck ten.
Its skin was very dusty,
It had a guitar that was rusty,
We played outside together,
But something happened to the weather.
He became very angry,
His poisonous hands were on me,
He wanted me to help him kill,
I didn't want to but I said, "I will
Find humans!"
They shook hands with Rocky's
Poisonous, ivy hands,
All dead!

Lois Allison (10)
Wilton Primary School, Hawick

The Rampage Of Bobzilla!

It comes from the underworld of my pants drawer,
And it only comes out
When I go to school.
It's spooky and poopy,
And it goes on a rampage all day long.
It's called Bobzilla,
Just like Godzilla,
But not so dramatic, funny and bad.
If you leave money, he'll take it all and spend it all,
It stays in my room, where else? Just my house,
But if you sneak quietly,
You can catch it with your pants!

Harris Jolly (9)
Wilton Primary School, Hawick

The Monster Called Kroda

From the Earth,
Comes a hairy dragon with lots of legs,
A dragon that has black wings,
And a green tail with blue eyes,
And it is super bad.
Kroda tries to kill everyone in the world,
He destroys all the houses in the world,
And if you try to kill him,
He will go into a smaller version of himself.

Thomas Ramage (9)
Wilton Primary School, Hawick

Xei Night

In a cupboard upstairs,
A creature is waiting,
For its next victim,
Be frightened.
At midnight, the creature goes wild,
It hunts for kids,
Flying miles and miles,
Maybe it will be at your house,
Next time!

Cerys Cumming (10)
Wilton Primary School, Hawick

YOUNG WRITERS INFORMATION

We hope you have enjoyed reading this book – and that you will continue to in the coming years.

If you're a young writer who enjoys reading and creative writing, or the parent of an enthusiastic poet or story writer, do visit our website **www.youngwriters.co.uk**. Here you will find free competitions, workshops and games, as well as recommended reads, a poetry glossary and our blog.

If you would like to order further copies of this book, or any of our other titles, then please give us a call or visit **www.youngwriters.co.uk**.

Young Writers
Remus House
Coltsfoot Drive
Peterborough
PE2 9BF
(01733) 890066
info@youngwriters.co.uk